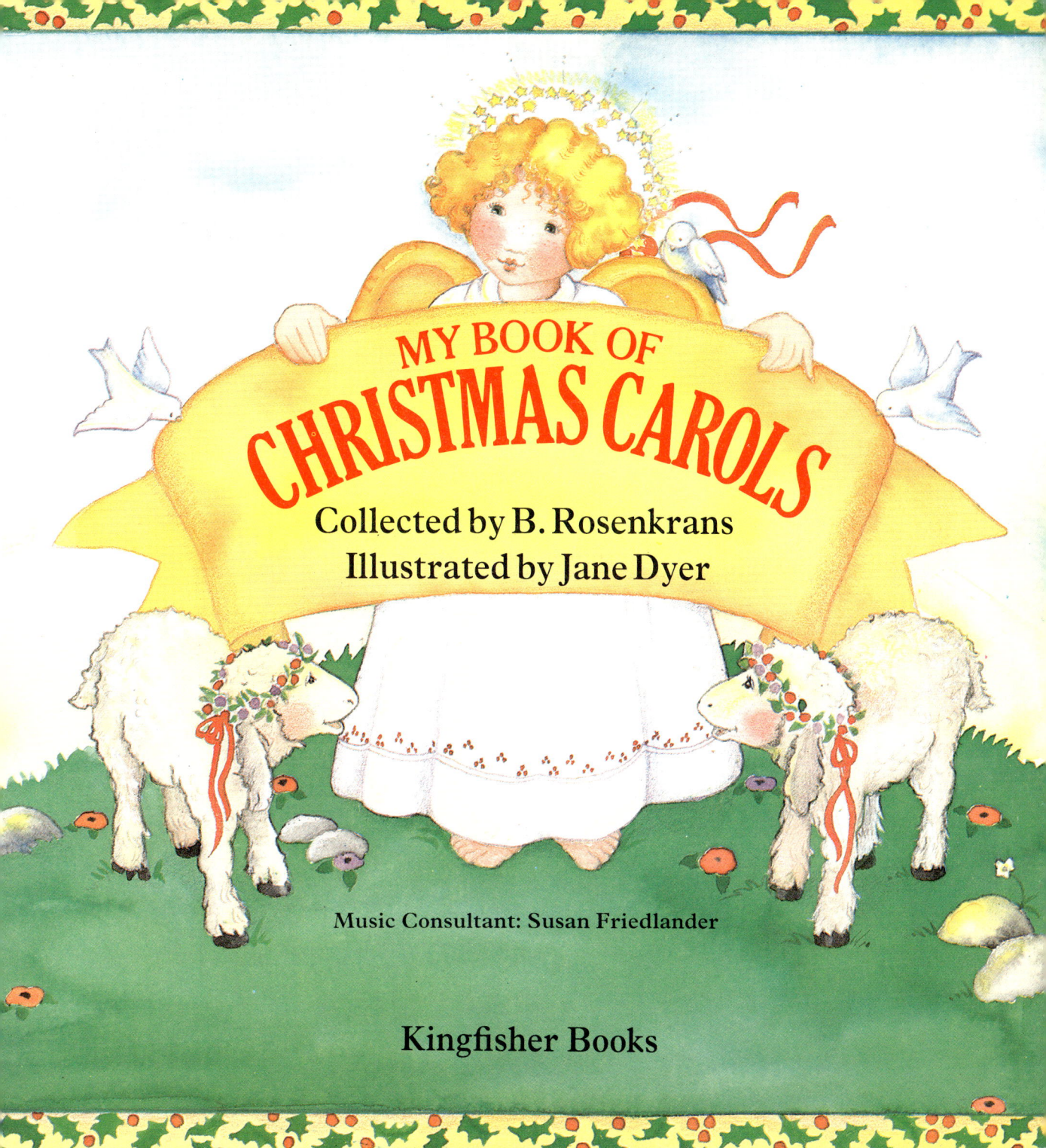

O COME, ALL YE FAITHFUL
(ADESTE FIDELES)

Probably dating from the seventeenth century, this hymn was sung in Latin for many, many years. Translated into English in the last century, it is still often heard in the Latin original.

English trans. by Rev. Frederick Oakeley, 1841

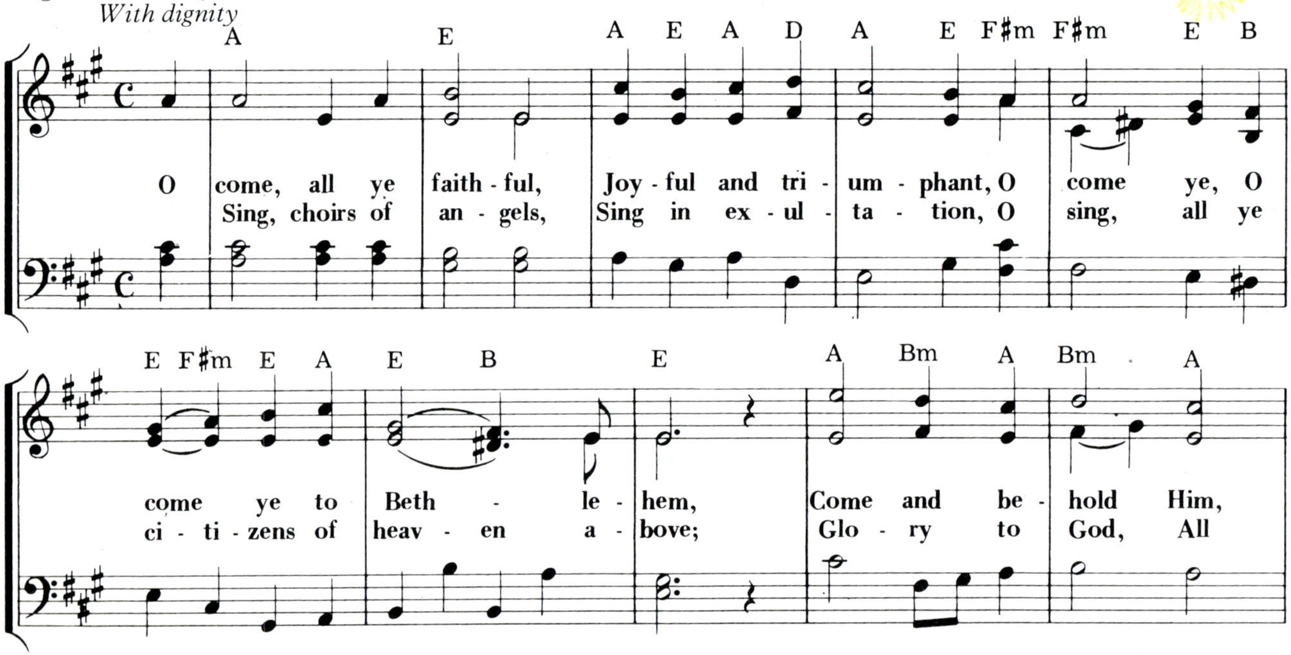

With dignity
A E A E A D A E F♯m F♯m E B
O come, all ye faith - ful, Joy - ful and tri - um - phant, O come ye, O
Sing, choirs of an - gels, Sing in ex - ul - ta - tion, O sing, all ye
E F♯m E A E B E A Bm A Bm A
come ye to Beth - le - hem, Come and be - hold Him,
ci - ti - zens of heav - en a - bove; Glo - ry to God, All

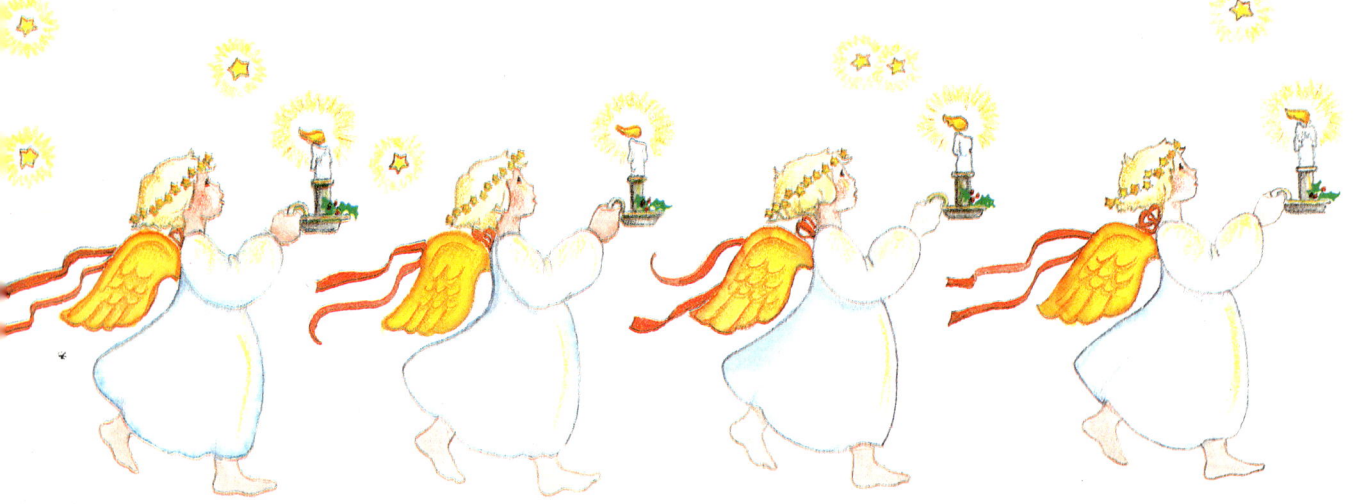

JOY TO THE WORLD!

The great English theologian and hymnist, Isaac Watts, based this hymn on the 98th psalm of the Old Testament.

For lo! the days are hast'ning on,
By prophets seen of old,
When with the ever circling years
Shall come the time foretold,
When the new heav'n and earth shall own
The Prince of Peace their King,
And the whole world send back the song
Which now the angels sing.

AWAY IN A MANGER

A sweet hymn once attributed to Martin Luther,
the song was long referred to as 'Luther's Cradle Hymn'.

Be near me, Lord Jesus,
I ask Thee to stay
Close by me for ever,
And love me, I pray;

Bless all the dear children
In Thy tender care,
And take us to heaven,
To live with Thee there.

DECK THE HALLS

A particularly joyous song, 'Deck the Halls' is a traditional Welsh carol.

Fast away the old year passes,
Fa la la la la, la la la la.
Hail the new, ye lads and lasses,
Fa la la la la, la la la la.
Sing we joyous all together,
Fa la la, la la la, la la la,
Heedless of the wind and weather,
Fa la la la la, la la la la.

O LITTLE TOWN OF BETHLEHEM

An American carol, thought to have been written on Christmas Eve by clergyman Phillips Brooks, and set to music by Lewis Redner, the church organist.

Phillips Brooks, 1868

Lewis H. Redner, 1868

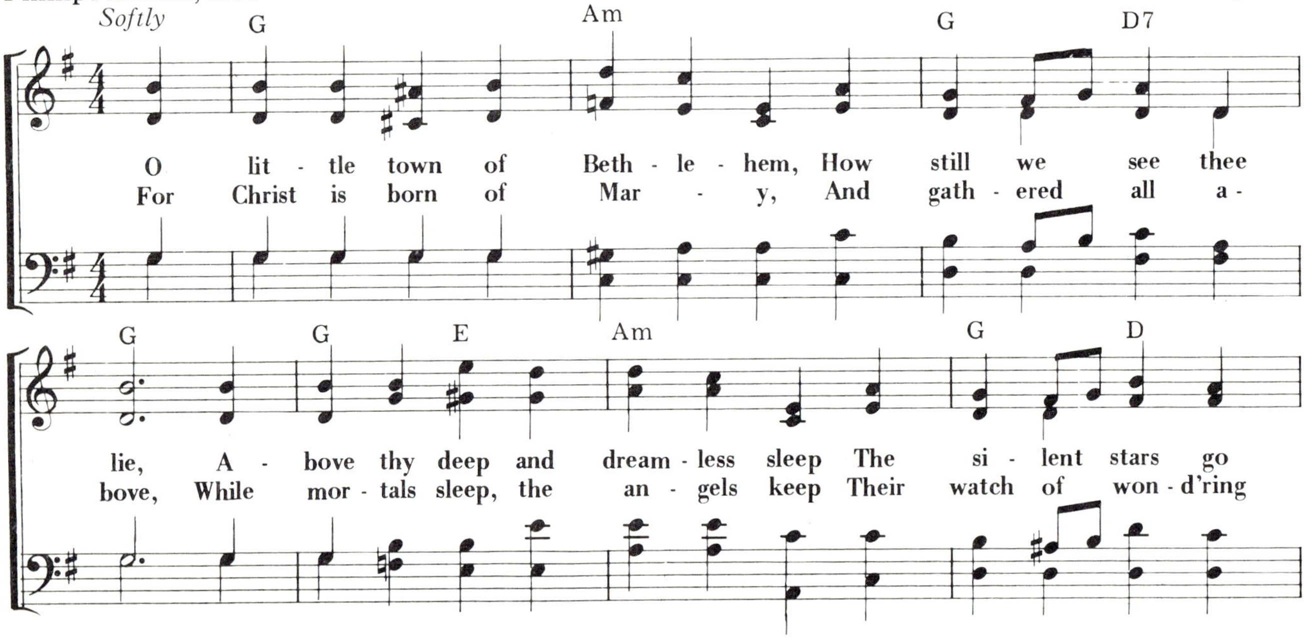
Softly
G Am G D7
O lit - tle town of Beth - le - hem, How still we see thee
For Christ is born of Mar - y, And gath - ered all a -
G G E Am G D
lie, A - bove thy deep and dream - less sleep The si - lent stars go
bove, While mor - tals sleep, the an - gels keep Their watch of won - d'ring

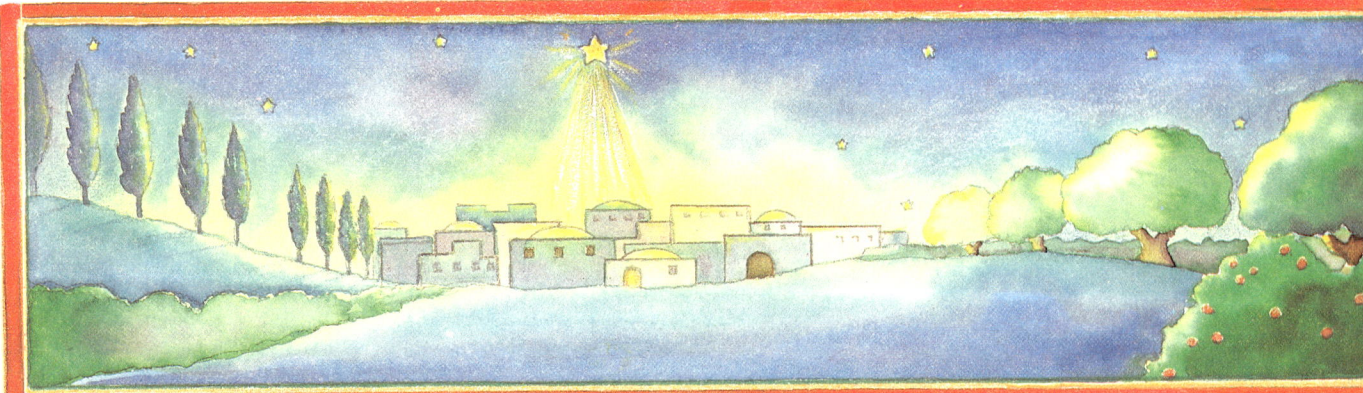

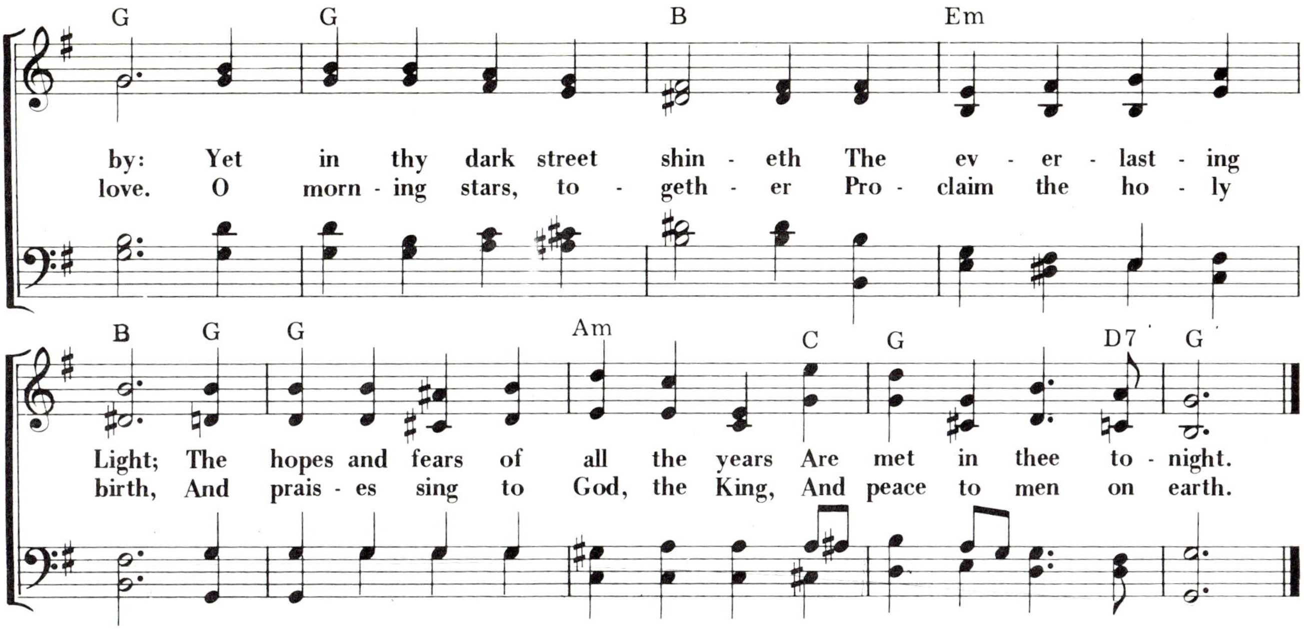
G G B Em
by: Yet in thy dark street shin - eth The ev - er - last - ing
love. O morn - ing stars, to - geth - er Pro - claim the ho - ly
B G G Am C G D7 G
Light; The hopes and fears of all the years Are met in thee to - night.
birth, And prais - es sing to God, the King, And peace to men on earth.

O holy Child of Bethlehem,
Descend to us, we pray;
Cast out our sin, and enter in,
Be born in us today.
We hear the Christmas angels
The great glad tidings tell;
O come to us, abide with us,
Our Lord Emmanuel.

How silently, how silently,
The wondrous gift is given;
So God imparts to human hearts
The blessing of His heaven.
No ear may hear His coming,
But in this world of sin,
Where meek souls will receive Him still,
The dear Christ enters in.

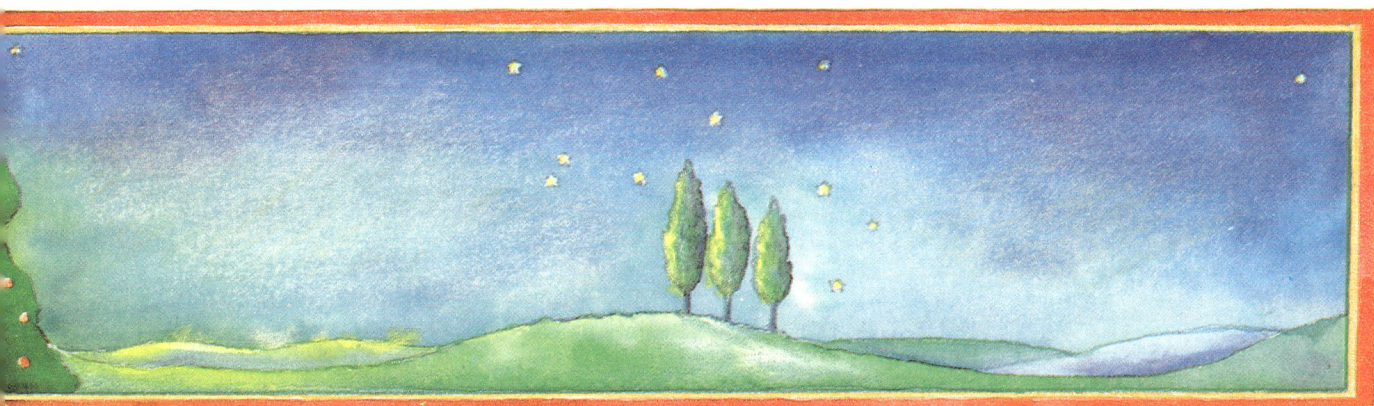

THE COVENTRY CAROL

This old English lullaby-carol is thought to have been used originally as part of a medieval Christmas pageant held in the city of Coventry.

O sisters, too, how may we do,
For to preserve this day;
This poor Youngling for whom we sing,
Bye, bye, lully, lullay.

Herod the King, in his raging,
Charged he hath this day
His men of might, in his own sight,
All children young to slay.

Then woe is me, poor Child, for thee,
And ever mourn and say,
For thy parting nor say nor sing,
Bye, bye, lully, lullay.

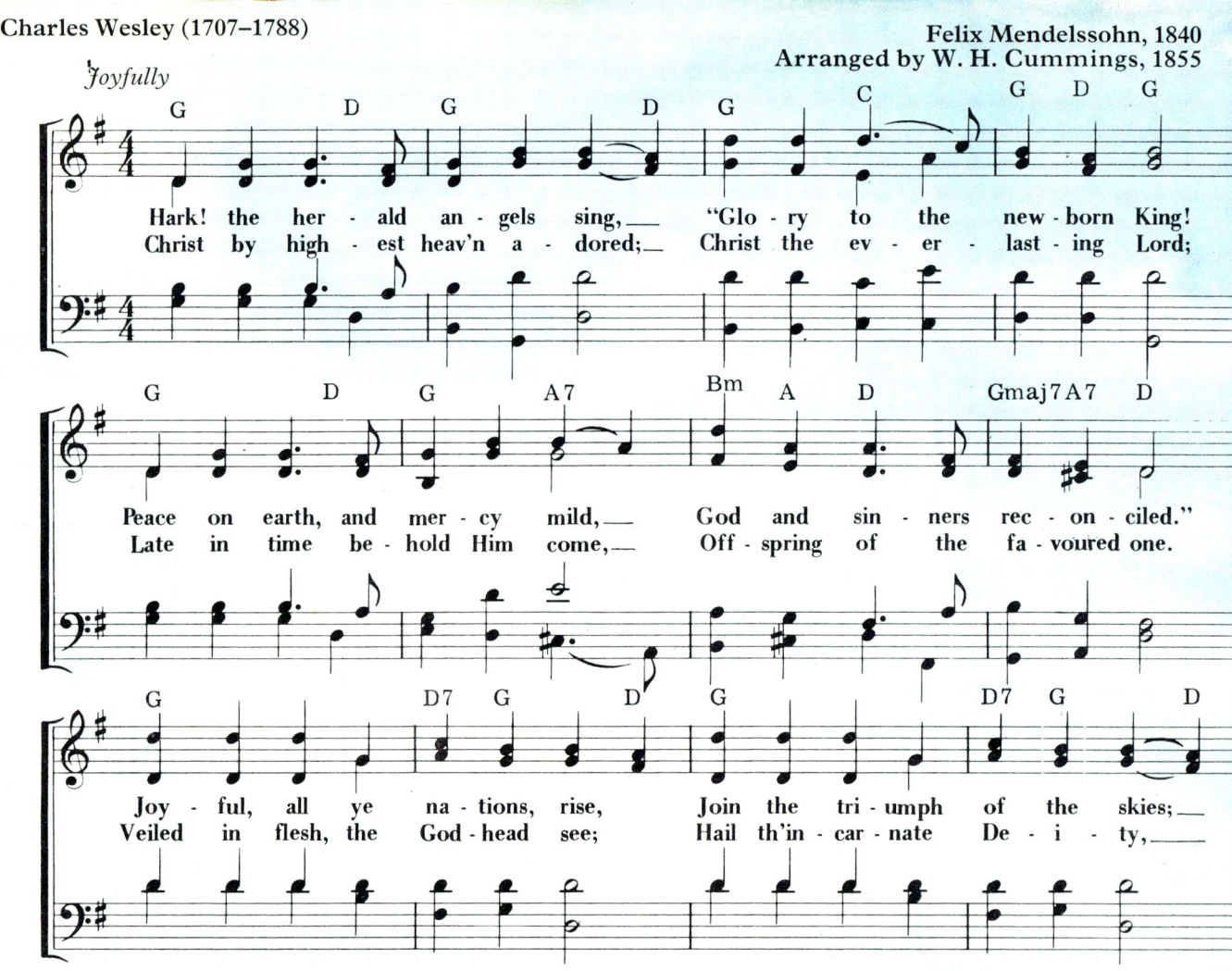

Gaspar:
Born a king on Bethlehem's plain,
Gold I bring to crown Him again;
King for ever, ceasing never,
Over us all to reign.
      CHORUS

Melchior:
Frankincense to offer have I,
Incense owns a Deity nigh,
Pray'r and praising, all men raising,
Worship Him, God on high.
      CHORUS

Balthasar:
Myrrh is mine; its bitter perfume
Breathes a life of gath'ring gloom;
Sorrowing, sighing, bleeding, dying,
Sealed in the stone-cold tomb.
      CHORUS

Glorious now behold Him arise,
King and God and Sacrifice;
Alleluia, Alleluia,
Earth to the heav'ns replies.
      CHORUS

WHAT CHILD IS THIS?

The melody for this carol is also known as 'Greensleeves'. It dates from at least the sixteenth century, although the tune was not used as the basis for a Christmas carol until much later.

William C. Dix (1837–1898)

Old English air
Arranged by Sir John Stainer

Moderately

What Child is this, who, laid to rest, On Mary's lap is sleeping? Whom angels greet with anthems sweet, While shepherds watch are keeping? This, this is Christ, the King, Whom shepherds guard and angels sing: Haste, haste to bring Him laud, The Babe, the Son of Mary.

So bring Him incense, gold, and myrrh, Come peasant, king to own Him; The King of kings salvation brings; Let loving hearts enthrone Him. Raise, raise the song on high, The Virgin sings her lullaby; Joy, joy for Christ is born, The Babe, the Son of Mary.

ANGELS WE HAVE HEARD ON HIGH

Also called the 'Angel's Hymn', the carol is sung to an old French melody and is considered to be one of the first Christmas hymns.

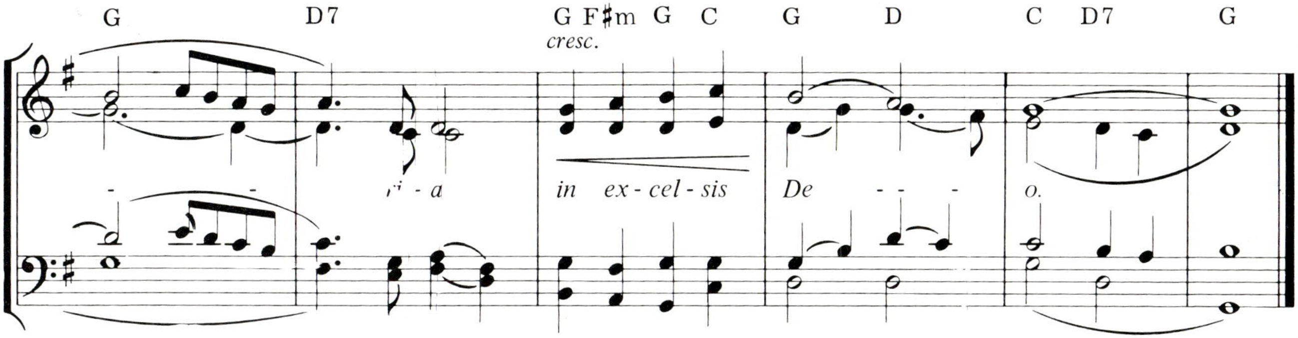

Come to Bethlehem and see
Him whose birth the angels sing;
Come adore on bended knee
Christ, the Lord, our newborn King.
        CHORUS

Shepherds, why this jubilee?
Why your joyous songs prolong?
What the gladsome tidings be,
Which inspire your heavenly song?
        CHORUS

SILENT NIGHT

This well-loved Austrian carol was written on Christmas Eve, 1818.

Joseph Möhr, 1818
Slowly and softly

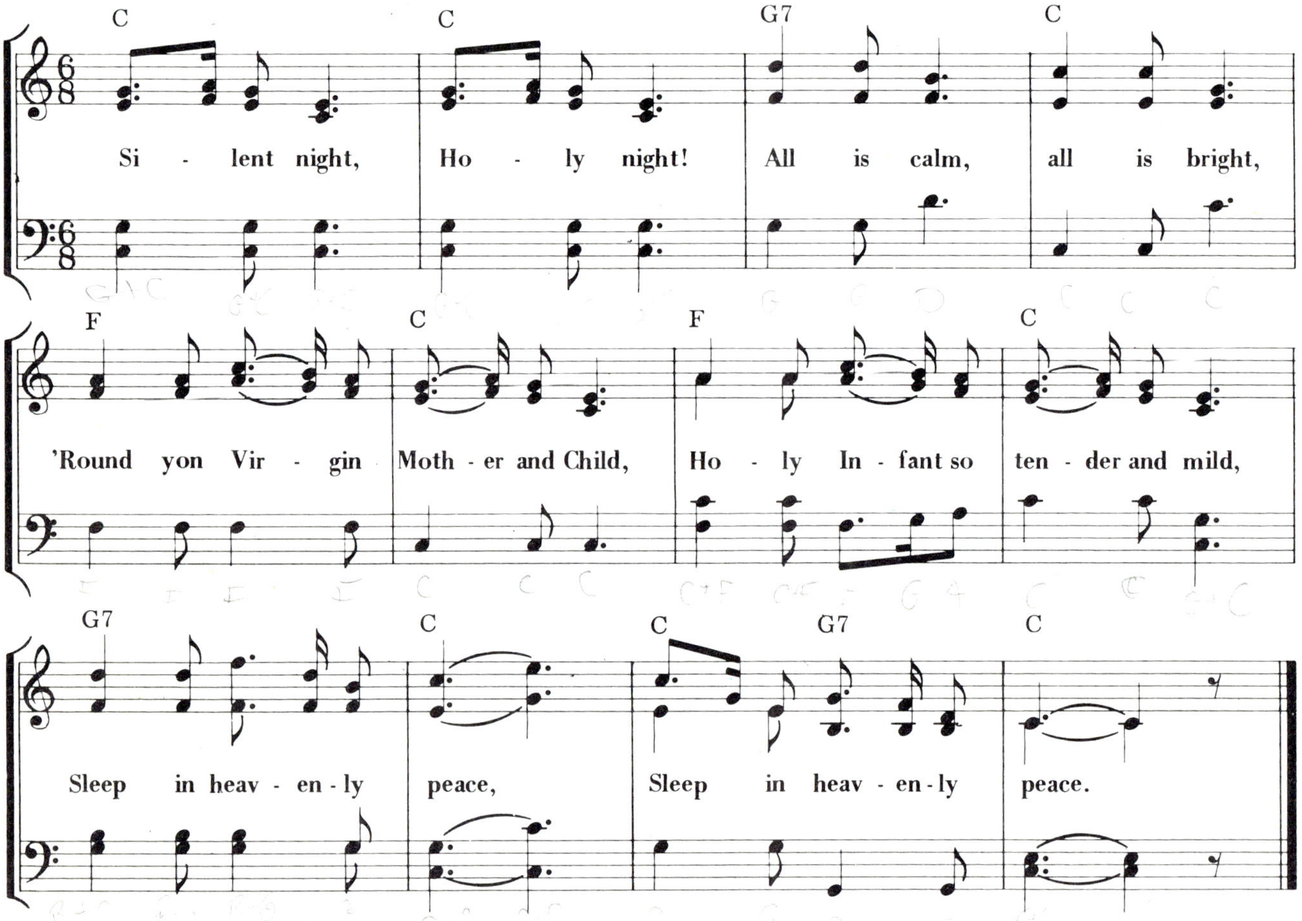

Franz Xavier Grüber, 1818

Si - lent night, Ho - ly night! All is calm, all is bright,

'Round yon Vir - gin Moth - er and Child, Ho - ly In - fant so ten - der and mild,

Sleep in heav - en - ly peace, Sleep in heav - en - ly peace.

Silent night, Holy night!
Shepherds quake at the sight!
Glories stream from heaven afar,
Heav'nly hosts sing, 'Alleluia!'
Christ, the Saviour, is born,
Christ, the Saviour, is born.

Silent night, Holy night!
Son of God, love's pure light,
Radiant beams from Thy Holy face,
With the dawn of redeeming grace,
Jesus, Lord, at Thy birth,
Jesus, Lord, at Thy birth.

INDEX OF CHRISTMAS CAROLS

Angels We Have Heard on High 28
Away in a Manger 10
Coventry Carol, The 16
Deck the Halls 12
First Noel, The.. 22
Hark! The Herald Angels Sing 18
It Came Upon a Midnight Clear 8
Jingle Bells 20
Joy to the World! 6
O Come, All Ye Faithful 4
O Little Town of Bethlehem 14
Silent Night.. 30
We Three Kings of Orient Are................ 24
What Child Is This? 26

Kingfisher Books, Grisewood & Dempsey Ltd,
Elsey House, 24–30 Great Titchfield Street, London W1P 7AD
This edition published in 1988 by Kingfisher Books.
Copyright © 1986 by Platt & Munk, Publishers,
A Division of Grosset & Dunlap, Inc.
Illustrations © 1986 by Jane Dyer
Published by arrangement with The Putnam Publishing Group, Inc.

All rights reserved. No part of this publication may be reproduced,
stored in a retrieval system or transmitted by any
means, electronic, mechanical, photocopying or
otherwise, without the prior permission of the publisher.
Printed in Spain

ISBN: 0 86272 336 1